NIETZSCHE'S HORSE

BY CHRISTOPHER KENNEDY

**Mitki/
Mitki**

North Carolina

First Edition

No part of this book may be reproduced without the written permission of
the publisher. Please direct inquiries to:

Mitki/Mitki Press
P.O. Box 570
Denver, NC 28037
http://www.mitkimitkipress.com
publisher@mitkimitkipress.com

ISBN 0-9707802-2-2

Cover designed by Drew Kenny.
Interior layout by Jeff Parker.
Printed and Bound in the United States of America.
This book is printed on acid-free paper.

The following poems appear or will appear in these publications, some in
slightly different form:

3rd Bed: "Decomposition #239" and "The Broken Lock"

Heliotrope: "Pets"

The Mississippi Review: "Three Stories"

For my daughters, Margeaux and Tessa, and for Steph,
whose love and friendship sustain me.

CONTENTS

You have wanted to pet all monsters.

—Nietzsche

1.

The First Real Televangelist

My father was a holy ghost. My mother a 20" Zenith. The progeny of religion and television, a machine with a soul, I wandered, unplugged, searching for a current. And when the neighbors asked me in, out of curiosity or spite, I plugged myself in and kept them entertained with visions of an electric heaven, a neon hell. When I signed off, I sang the national anthem, led them in a prayer, and as the star-spangled banner unfurled across my chest they'd stand and salute, say what a good boy I was.

I can't say exactly when it turned bad. Their faces as they stared began to have the quality of raw meat, marbled slabs caught in the false reverie of my cathode ray rapture. I could feel myself becoming human, the sharp edges of my cabinet rounding out, muscles and tissue where I once held transistors.

When emotions crept in, I knew I was finished. Pity came first, then all the other annihilating Truths. So when I finished my last performance at the Golden Age of Television Tent Revival Meeting, I shed my first tear and said a prayer under my breath for the sold-out crowd as I pulled the plug on myself, ashamed of mine own America.

It's Nice Inside The Labyrinth

After the minotaur's timely or untimely death, depending on your perspective, the new occupant, a pleasant mythological creature named Stan, who had a human head, an elephant's body, a kangaroo's hind legs, and an ostrich's vestigial wings, set up home. He brought his prints with him and hung them on the walls: Mondrian; Picasso; Miro; Chagall. He loved them all, and though it took a few years for him to be sure he'd hung prints on every wall, he couldn't rest until the place felt "homey." Of course, in the process, he discovered exactly how to get in and out of the labyrinth in a few minutes. So he could leave at any time, but he decided it was nice inside the labyrinth and stayed. Those who were sentenced to wander there agreed with Stan, and it was inevitable that once they met him they'd become friends.

At Stan's parties, the guests, or the condemned as they liked to refer to themselves, would see who could get to the exit of the labyrinth the quickest. But they'd always go back to the party, reporting their time to Stan, who was busy arranging finger sandwiches on a silver tray or tasting a new pâté.

Eventually, word of Stan's parties got to the king, and he entered the labyrinth himself to check out his information. *Nice pad, Stan*, said the king, when he saw all the modern art on the walls. And this is how the modern world came into being. Not at all scary, not at all as serious as you might think.

Personality Quiz

Q: How would you describe your ability to work with others?
A: A lost shoe in a forest.

Q: Who is the person you would most like to emulate?
A: A photograph locked in a trunk.

Q: How would you characterize yourself in an emergency situation?
A: A child lost in a maze.

Q: What is your most interesting quality?
A: A half-finished painting in an attic.

Q: Which celebrity would you like to portray you in the story of your life?
A: An exterminator, carrying a spider outdoors to safety.

Q: Is there anything about yourself you would change?
A: A broken lock on a door.

Q: Anything else?
A: A missing windowpane.

Q: How would you like to be remembered after your death?
A: The answer to a question no one asks.

Q: What is your favorite television show?
A: A windmill on fire in a young girl's dream.

Q: If you could be another animal, what would you be?
A: A slab of meat on a conveyer belt, receiving a soul.

Q: How would you describe yourself to others?
A: The problem and the solution.

Q: How would others describe you?
A: A shadow hidden in the shade.

Q: How would you describe your state of mind?
A: A curious beachcomber, glimpsing a tidal wave.

Q: Do you have an ideal vacation spot?
A: The early test sites in Nevada.

Q: Is there a person from your past who has made an impression on you?
A: A priest in line for confession.

Q: If you were an inanimate object, what would you be?
A: 30 degrees latitude, dreaming it's the equator.

Q: How would you describe your social life?
A: A monk on his deathbed with a vision of sex.

Q: How would you describe your time management skills?
A: An hourglass lost in the desert.

Q: Who is your hero?
A: A fish that's developed a fear of drowning.

Q: How would you describe your religious beliefs?
A: A dyslexic psychic, predicting the past.

Three Stories

Van Gogh's Ear

I found van Gogh's ear in a box of cereal. I poured the
cereal into a bowl, and there amid the flakes and raisins lay
the ear. At first, I didn't recognize it. I thought it might be
a piece of dried fruit, fig or apricot. But when I picked it
up and held it in the palm of my hand, I knew it was an
ear. Now, I had to decide whose ear. I ruled out Getty's
grandson. It was too big, as his, I remembered, was curled
and small like a snail. No, it was Vincent's ear, ant-crawled,
decomposing, listening, perhaps, to the (metallic) sound of
God's voice. Delicate layers of skin, wrinkled and peeling,
until all that was left was a soft cartilage. I put it back in
the bowl and poured on the milk. Then there was the
matter of a spoon.

Novel

My love affair with tapioca ended as quickly as it began. It
was, and still is I suppose, varicose veins that ruined the
marriage. Methuselah loved the lake in winter. I was as
lonely as Emily Dickinson's gynecologist.

I'll never forget the man with one finger who looked me in
the eye and said, *Maybe if you cut your hair, you wouldn't
look so much like Francis Bacon.*

The smell of formaldehyde, that's what I'll remember best,
the antiseptic glow, the Nuremberg in her eyes. That

Hermione should choose to marry a moose was no surprise, accepted even. *But why this moose?* wondered her mother, the matted hair, the stench. She didn't object so much as raise her nose whenever he walked in the room.

Good evening, Mr. and Mrs. Swedish Ambassador, I do hope you enjoyed the music of the flies! exclaimed the Antichrist.

Would Nathan accept the slanted way she walked? The detective noticed. The detective knew all the facts. He slid his notebook inside his coat. He observed the hibiscus flowering in the south end garden. The tumescent buds; the sensation of never again.

The retrograde motion of the planets brought them all into alignment. The parlor seemed a logical place for the enmity to spill over into the soufflé. *Would you care for some Hollandaise with your asparagus? I don't know why it means so much to me if you do.*

That was the last formal remark from our hostess. She was seen again, hovering near the light fixture, attenuated and cherub-cheeked.

Art Class

In religion class we had to draw a picture of Christ on the cross. I was drawing and coloring my picture of Christ and holding it up away from myself at arm's length to admire it when my teacher, Sister Mary C., walked over to my desk and snatched the picture out of my hand. She yelled at me and told me to start over and to stop being disrespectful. I didn't understand why she was mad, but all the other kids in the class were laughing at me, which was a good sign they knew what I had done wrong. After class, I asked my friend, D., who was the best artist in the class, what I had done wrong. He said I made Christ look fat and bald. I said that Christ probably was fat and bald. He said it didn't matter, that Christ always looks like a tall, thin guy with long hair, sort of like a rock star. Anyway, that's the only experience with art that I can remember, and it wasn't very pleasant. I don't like feeling stupid, and art makes me feel stupid most of the time.

The Bird Man of Albatross

I gathered a few twigs and some Styrofoam. I combed
through garbage cans and found some string and a woman's
auburn hair. I carried these things to the top of a tree.
There, I built my nest and waited to attract a female of the
species.

If I were a bird, I'd be the envy of the neighborhood. As it
is, I'm a man. A bird man, perhaps, but still a man. I
practiced my call, a guttural trill, followed by a high-
pitched chortle and a soliloquy in the lower registers:
Richard Burton reading from the phone book on the Mike
Douglas Show.

You'd be surprised how many women looked my way,
though never face to face or eye to eye. Which reminds me:
a bird's eye view has its advantages. I see the whole picture,
and my feathers get ruffled never. I know where things are
headed. My nest fits one nicely.

Lucky

As he received his change from the drugstore cashier, he noticed a silver dollar among the smaller coins. *This is my lucky dollar,* he said to his daughter, and he put it in his pocket. The next day when he put on a clean pair of pants, he remembered the dollar and though he never thought of himself as a superstitious man, he reached into the pocket of his jeans, took out the dollar, and slid it into his pants pocket.

On the drive to work, he was involved in a fender bender and was late for work. Some lucky coin, was his first thought, but his second thought, which he considered the more profound, was how much worse the accident could have been. Maybe there was something to this lucky coin thing after all.

From then on, he continued to keep the dollar in his pocket, and each day, no matter what bad thing happened to him, he was convinced the coin had kept whatever it was from being worse. So, for example, when his house burned down, he held the coin in his hand as he stood in his front yard, watching the house collapse into itself like a wounded buffalo, thinking how fortunate he was to have survived and to have saved his stamp collection and parakeet.

One day, as he was walking home to his new apartment in a run down neighborhood after seeing a terrible movie, though not as terrible as it might have been, he was approached by a gang of teen-agers and chased into a building on the campus of the local university. Once inside the building, he ran into a room and shut the door. The dimpled, pale green glass of the door had red letters written across it. He had a hard time reading what they were, especially with the shadows of the gang members flickering across the glass as they waited for him to come out.

But once he regained his composure, he read the warning: DANGER: HAZARDOUS MEDICAL WASTE. DO NOT ENTER. The man sat down on a metal chair with wheels and slid backwards, took a deep, toxic breath of incurable viral strains, and reached into his pocket. *God*, he said, *I'd hate to think what things would be like without my lucky coin.*

The Man Who Invented Hunger

He had finally had enough. His stomach had shrunk to the size of a lima bean. All his internal organs resembled eggplants and pomegranates. His eyes were two olives. He began to devour himself, starting with his feet and eating his way to the top of his head. The more he ate, the hungrier he became. Each piece of him stimulated a craving for another piece.

In a matter of minutes, he was gone. When he finished, all that was left was a skeleton and the original hunger.

Social Anxiety Disorder

I wandered for three days in bed under the covers. I slept in a desert and hoped water would appear. I wondered if the sand was really as hot as it looked. Yesterday, I even forgot to breathe. The horse that rode with me began to cry. I didn't have the heart to witness such a tragedy, so I shot him. I dragged his carcass across the desert in search of the elusive mirage. The traffic heading the other way was miserable. Although all of them had hopeful looks on their faces and averted their eyes when they saw which way I was headed. The horse grew heavier even as the vultures stripped his flesh. Pretty soon all I was dragging was a horse's skull and a single vulture. I entered the oasis that way and had trouble making friends at first.

Gem of a Woman

For twenty-three years a man collects gems of every sort: diamonds; emeralds; rubies; opals; sapphires; and amethysts. He finally decides he has enough to begin his project. He builds a woman out of the jewels. He calls her Doris. He asks Doris to marry him. She says yes, although he has to provide her with a voice since she is actually an inanimate object and hasn't one of her own.

The marriage lasts for thirty years, until the man dies. On his deathbed he asks Doris to promise she will never marry again. In a feeble, resigned voice she says yes. After the man dies, Doris sits at home until the mailman notices all the mail that has piled up, opens the door and sees Doris and her dead husband. He calls an ambulance and they take the body to the morgue. The mailman is so taken with Doris that he proposes on the spot. She says yes in spite of her promise to her first husband, although the mailman provides the voice for her, an eager, anticipatory voice, breathy and deep.

Another thirty years go by and the mailman makes the same request as the first husband. Doris responds in the same feeble, resigned voice that she will indeed remain faithful to the mailman.

For several decades, Doris marries, is widowed, and marries again and again. Her husbands range in age from nineteen to eighty-three. Some of the men are wealthy, some poor. Some are handsome, some distinctly unattractive. Doris doesn't seem to care about superficial things. She loves them all equally. She is the perfect wife.

Eventually, she ends up in a museum and marries the curator. It's a small wedding. Just a few friends and relatives. All on the curator's side. And they, too, will live happily ever after. A work of art and a man who can appreciate such things.

Pleasure

To please Death, I smeared lamb's blood on my face to gather a beard of flies. I slaughtered a pig and hung its entrails from a hook around my neck. I fashioned a purse from the pig's head and stuffed it with dollar bills.

A woman told me she liked the way my mind works. I said, *When the squirrel runs the wheel everything's fine, but when he stops, I get a little nuts.* She said she had second thoughts. I said, *When the squirrel gets hungry, watch out.* She said she had to go now. I said, *Do you have any squirrel feed on you?* She said it was getting late. I said, *You shouldn't start something you can't finish.*

Then, to please Death again, I chopped off my arm and put it in the freezer. I seared the wound shut with a steam iron and learned the sound of one hand clapping.

The woman left unceremoniously. I left to the fanfare of trumpets and the applause of rare roast beef.

2.

Song of the Local Economy

A sinister absence of primary colors—buildings rise and
fall; businesses collapse and head south for cheap labor. All
the citizens wear nametags and hats shaped like vacuum
cleaner bags. Yesterday, the department stores announced a
sale on everything: buy one, get the manager's first born
free. Rumplestiltskin would love this town. The Chamber
of Commerce is empty. The Knights of Columbus have
been devoured by dragons. On a more personal note: I am
homeless in my home. I have filed for moral bankruptcy.
Any minute now, I expect to be elected mayor. My first
piece of legislation: to declare myself a disaster area, let the
federal government take care of me. The new American
dream, I sleepwalk toward the door, my zipper at half-mast.
I promise to make good on all my promises. One problem:
I seem to have misplaced my speech.

The Unforgivable Silence

He was a man of odd proportions. His feet were the size of canoes; his head the size of a small lemon. His arms were approximate to the size of two spatulas. *You will find the woman of your dreams,* his mother said whenever the man of odd proportions cried in his sleep. *You have inner beauty,* she whispered in his minuscule ears.

After his mother died, the man stuffed her into a garbage bag and dragged her out to the patio. She lay there the entire winter, while her son sat on the couch, bathed in the sanctifying blue light of television. The television became like a funhouse mirror, distorting the man's sense of self until he imagined himself to be like the actors he saw, as if he were somehow alive inside the television like a salamander in a terrarium, his life a fantasy of cathode ray-inspired delusion.

But televisions are no substitute for a home-cooked meal and a clean bathroom, so he began to miss his mother and shouted her name. *Mother,* he bellowed, and his voice echoed down the long hallway toward her bedroom. He kept shouting for what seemed like hours and drifted off to sleep in the recliner.

He dreamed of her, standing over him, whispering a kindness into his perversely tiny ears, the woman of his dreams.

Dali's Ants Visit My Living Room, Wearing Tiny Togas

Just as I'm thinking, *Someone else owns this planet,* they arrive, single file, crawling along the woven edge of the wicker wastebasket. Spread out methodically, a phalanx of such precision they must be Spartans. With marbles between their pincers, they begin to speak, their squeaky tenors a univocal chorus of admonitions. *What Greeks are these?* I ask, and their only answer is to form the word Demosthenes.

Look, I say, *here come the Persians, all 10, 000 of them;* better fasten our chin straps, polish the shields they'll carry us home on, odds against us, guarding the passage between this world and the next, the future of Western civilization at stake, and those damn Athenians, late with their ships as usual.

The Coroner's Surprise

It was a huge, gift-wrapped box that sat on one of the slabs for weeks, until one Friday when the coroner announced he would open it later that afternoon. There was such anticipation from the morgue workers that the place took on an almost festive air. Some even wore party hats and blew into noisemakers. Quite an accomplishment for a workplace known for its stiffs. Just before it was time to go home, the coroner called everyone to the slab. He tore open the box and said *Ta da!* One of the workers said *Hey, it's just another dead guy.* Yes, said the coroner, *but this one's my father,* and the workers clapped and remarked how they'd never had such a nice surprise.

Bad Luck Since The Age of Reason

A man wraps the chalk outline of his violent death around his neck like a white scarf; a woman marries her reflection and shortly after files for divorce. The god of Love misses them both with his paltry arrows. *I'm not what I used to be*, he says, *but then, neither are my targets. You can say that again*, whisper the gods of Truth and Beauty.

In a small town behind a mountain, a boy and a girl fall in love without any help from outside influences. The villagers quickly stone them to death. Some years later, a man carves a statue: the lovers in a staid embrace, accepting their fate in each other's arms. The sculptor, moved by his own creation, dies of a broken heart. The statue is placed at the foot of his grave, a monument, or, as the mayor said at the dedication, a warning to those who stray.

Approaching the Fire

The fire refused to burn out. As it was the only fire in the house, and as it was the only house the family owned, there was much discussion of what to do. *Water's too good for it,* shouted the excitable father. *What would Jesus do?* asked the religious mother. The young one was in the kitchen, asking the oven for insight.

Love Song of the Autodidact

Whatever I know about love I taught myself. I was raised
by a few employees in a shopping mall. My favorite
waitress wore pink. My favorite manager wore short sleeved
shirts in winter. For argument's sake, I'll call them mom
and dad.

I had more televisions than fingers, a row of them in the
department store. I tell you, I invented intertextuality in
Sears & Roebuck, September 8, 1966.

I lived on a steady diet of Mallo Cups and taught strangers
how to pick the right banana to win a banana split.

It's always 72 degrees in heaven and Fairmount Fair. I still
covet the blue Fender Stratocaster in the window of The
Music Box. I stood for hours in front of Noah's Ark,
watching the three-toed sloths. My life creeping along like
their hirsute bodies. Whenever I see a terrarium, I know
exactly how it feels to be inside.

Whatever I know about love I taught myself. Attention
shoppers: there's a blue light special in aisle eleven, a clean
up in aisle number two.

Nietzsche's Horse

When the whip came down from out of the white sun, he
wrapped his arms around my neck, then whispered in my
ear. Such brilliance, even a horse could understand. For a
moment, when he clung to me, we were a god, half-man,
half-beast, a genius of muscle and thought.

I rode off under my cruel master's hand; he walked off
under his.

3.

Spritual

A man, who shall remain nameless, mostly because his parents were lazy and indecisive, spends the day in some nervous god's sweaty palm. A feeling of sadness envelops him, but he feels safe in a strangely disconcerting way. He walks out to the edge of the god's longest finger to see if he can get a look at the god's face. The god looks exactly like the man, but because the face is so big, the man doesn't notice, and he begins trying to match up the features— prominent nose, cleft chin—with gods he knows from other religions. He's stumped. *Must be from some mythology I'm not familiar with*, he surmises.

As the day wears on, he feels sadder and less safe. What if the god gets hungry? Isn't the man likely to be the most convenient snack? He remembers one of those stories in Greek mythology where some god or giant eats all his kids. *And we're not even related*, he thinks, now more afraid than ever.

He walks out to the end of the finger again and waves to the god. The god lowers his hand down to the floor and the man climbs off. Nothing is said, and the man walks away. As he is walking he turns back toward the god and immediately recognizes that the god looks exactly like him. *I thought a god would be better looking*, he mumbles to himself and walks home.

You'll never guess what happened to me, he says to his wife. *Don't tell me. You spent the day in the sweaty palm of some nervous god who looks just like you. How'd you guess?* he asks. *I saw it on television. You're famous. Well, I'll be damned*, he says. *That's what they said on TV*, the wife says.

And now he knows there must be more to the story.

Word Problem

Train A leaves Cleveland at 2:00 p.m. EST, heading south-west at 60 mph, carrying thirty-four passengers, seven of whom share the same first name, driven by a color-blind engineer, whose pulse rate is 120 beats per minute, and who has recently left his wife for a younger woman, age 27, who has two sisters who live in Des Moines.

Train B leaves St. Louis at 4:00 p.m. CT, heading northeast at 75 mph, carrying forty-nine passengers, three of whom played second base for the Cardinals, driven by a dyslexic engineer, who recently made a nine day pilgrimage to Lourdes and has twelve or twenty-one children, and wishes, in either case, not to have anymore.

Assuming the trains are on the same track, how long will it take before they collide?

Why does the woman in seat 27A of train B survive when everyone else dies?

Was human error to blame or divine intervention?

For each equation, let X equal infinity.

Please read the questions carefully. Remember, there are many good answers, some better than others, but there is only one correct answer to each question.

Take as much time as you need. Keep in mind, the next section is much harder.

Good luck. You may begin.

Old Neighborhood

A middle-aged man visits his old neighborhood. Now that he's older, he thinks the hills will seem smaller. In fact, the hills are higher than ever, steeper than before. He has to place his hands on his knees to keep walking. It's a strain, but he reaches the top of the hill his old house is on.

The house is a hundred times bigger than he remembered it. The door is plain white with three windows, each pane slightly lower than the one before it. He can't reach the doorknob; the welcome mat is the size of an Olympic swimming pool. He taps on the door and a giant woman who looks like his mother answers.

I used to live here, he shouts up to his giant mother. But she can't see or hear him and closes the door. He walks back down the hill toward the house he lives in now. Suddenly, the hills in his current neighborhood seem higher and steeper than before.

When he reaches his house it is a hundred times bigger than it was when he left. He doesn't bother trying to open the door. He figures a giant woman who looks like his wife will answer, and she won't be able to see or hear him.

He decides to look for a new neighborhood, someplace scaled more to his liking. All the hills are very steep. He's pretty sure nothing is going to be the same.

The Broken Lock

The family sat down to dinner. The mother led them in saying grace. *...and to my oldest son, I say, I eat the dust of your leaving.* Then, the uncomfortable silence. After dinner, their separate rooms were on fire of a different sort. There were only two of them. A mother and a son. All night, the wind spread the flames, but no one noticed, or if they did, no one cared to call out. Though, in their defense, fire is often invisible, a pale blue flame and a crackling sound like a broken lock on an empty gun cabinet.

Incapable of Being Elsewhere

A pair of black, high-heeled, velvet shoes decided to leave the feet they were on and make a new life for themselves. They made it as far as the side of a highway on-ramp and stopped, unsure which way to go. One shoe faced east and west, while the other faced north and south.

As cars drove past, the drivers made up stories about the shoes. One driver imagined an abduction, the shoes falling off as the woman was pulled into a large, late model luxury car, possibly a Cadillac or a Lincoln Continental.

Another driver saw a suitcase tied to the luggage rack on a wood-paneled station wagon, a Ford or a Chevy, and the suitcase opening, but only the shoes tumbling out, the clothes having been secured by elastic straps.

Still another driver pictured a lovers quarrel, the woman hiking up her evening gown as she walked along the side of the road, then taking off each shoe and heaving them, one at a time, at her boyfriend. They were probably more than a little drunk, he thought as he sped away toward his job.

The catalysts for these dramas remained situated on the shoulder of the road, contemplating their next move, which for some reason they couldn't seem to motivate themselves to attempt, and so they began to make up stories about the cars that drove by them and about the drivers, each in a little world of his or her own, incapable of being elsewhere.

Aerial View

From the waiting room window, the highways express their purpose geometrically, even aesthetically. They curve and spiral, run straight into the distance, then disappear. The word *spoke* comes to mind. Bicycle wheels; wheelchairs. Is this a progression, a riddle for the sphinx?

Most likely it's the killing of time. And the cars form orderly rows of traffic. Primary colors, mostly. Imports. And here he's reminded of ribbon candy. It was like eating a mixture of sugar and glass. Grandmother a murderer? Who knows?

From here, he can almost love the anonymous drivers. From where they are they can't know much about where they're going. Where he is is a good distance away, a view he's come to enjoy.

In a few minutes, when the doctor asks him what's wrong, he'll tell him: Memory is a bad dream that won't let me sleep. He'll assume a regal pose, aloof and knowing. Like God in heaven, he'll point out the window toward the ground as if toward the past.

See, he'll say, *from here it all makes sense.*

Sideshow of Good Intentions

In this tent, the Sword Swallower attempts to slide a long
series of words down his throat, each letter barbed with
anguish and regret. The crowd winces as vowels and
consonants disappear into his mouth. His humility
astounds them, their own bravado drained. Next, the 500
lbs. woman resists the temptation to order dessert, causing
the Strong Man to weep, revealing his sensitive side.
Finally, the Hermaphrodite resolves its gender differences
without a net. The battle of the sexes is over, and the men
and women in the crowd inch closer to one another,
holding hands as they parade down the midway toward the
strip joint.

But when the saxophone begins its sexy wail, and Trixie
L'Amour tugs at the fingers of her silver gloves, the crowd
senses something is wrong: without difference nothing is
erotic. Trixie, feeling she's lost her touch, storms off the
stage and opens a home for wayward women as the crowd
heads for the exit, complaining bitterly about the high cost
of entertainment these days.

Darwin's Last Stand

Through some mistake of evolution, a man inherited a
monkey's brain and a magpie's soul. To put it another way:
he had neither brain nor soul big enough for his body to
bear. He went about his business. He got a job at the
banana factory, went to church on Sunday and sat way in
the back, nodding out during the sermon.

He had a neighbor who felt something was not right with
him. The neighbor went to the police. He reported the
man as deficient in ways that were hard to comprehend.
That was enough for the police. They arrested the man. He
was tried and convicted of being an anomaly.

He went to prison. The other prisoners left him alone.
They sensed something was wrong with him, and besides,
they didn't know what an anomaly was, but they didn't
want to find out, either.

After forty years of good behavior, he was released. He
stood outside the prison gate and began to weep. He could
see, what with everyone's knuckles almost touching the
ground, that after four decades, people had begun to catch
up. *My species,* he said to himself, *my species.*

The Most Important Meal of the Day

The child Savior's face appeared in my Western omelet. I asked the waitress to verify the miracle. *Sorry, sir,* she said, *I'm agnostic.* I complained to the manager. *My cream is curdled,* I screamed. *That's cottage cheese,* came his curt reply.

Just when it seemed over, the von Trapp family singers, pursued by Nazis, crossed the Alps into the foyer of the restaurant and yodeled the theme from *The Untouchables.*

When the cops arrived, I explained it was all a misunderstanding. *Had I known I was seated in the non-believers section, I'd have kept my mouth shut,* I said to the largest officer.

The handcuffs were tight around my wrists, but I didn't flinch. Though once restrained in the back of the cruiser, I wept all the way to the Vatican.

Music of the Spheres

The List of Possible Thirds

For a while, I had the distinct impression I was Jesus
Christ. Not an uncommon occurrence in my neighborhood
after the white mescaline made its rounds. I set about to
convert the non-believers, but all I could find was other
Christs. I knew them by their given names as they knew
me by mine, but we were all convinced of our divinity.
There was nothing to do except form a committee. We met
twice a week to discuss theology and smoke hash oil. A few
friends sought me out. They were two and needed one.
They made a list of possible thirds. When the phone rang,
I thought it was the doctor, returning my call. *Are you
hearing things?* they asked. *Are you seeing things?* I had heard
Gregorian chants. I had seen ants crawl in and out of my
mouth, carrying crumbs to their queen. I lied and said no.
A few months later, I was talking with another friend who
told me about the list, their plan to form a trinity. There
were several names, but mine was at the top. Apparently,
had I been honest, the three of us would have ushered in ·
the end of the world. This was in '77, right about the time
I was getting into punk.

Hamelin

I found a stick on my way to the boathouse. A handsome
stick torn from the branches of a red maple and rid of all its
annoying leaves. I took it home and dressed it in my
daughter's doll clothes. I especially liked its little red cap. It
slept in my bed with me and never snored. We lived this

way for a few weeks, until my neighbor made an inappro-
priate remark. I stripped the stick of its clothes and
sharpened it with a steak knife. Now it was a weapon, and
I plunged it deep into my neighbor's heart. I pulled it out,
dripping with neighbor blood, and wiped it off. I brought
it inside and carved out its middle. I poked some holes in it
and sanded its mouth down to a reed-like opening. I played
a song on my new flute to celebrate my recent victory. I
walked to the edge of town, followed by all the filthiest
vermin, and became a legend. That's the part people
remember.

The Half-Blue House

As if the house had fallen asleep, the family inside a dream.
In one of the bedrooms, the Fugs sang "Wet Dreams Over
You." An animal corpse decomposed in the basement like
melting snow. The machines all had wheels, and there were
many machines. The father knew about them, but he sat
all day at the dining room table, smoking unfiltered
cigarettes. His t-shirt was dingy yellow under the arms.
The two sons owned several guns and a bow and arrow set.
Toward the end of the dream, the older son went to prison
as an accomplice to murder. The younger son drowned in
the reservoir at sixteen. He had recently learned how to
play the drums. There was a great deal of sex going on in
there, but not the kind you would ever tell anyone about.
The neighbors agreed it was a shame the older son's
girlfriend was pregnant. The fetus trembled whenever her
potential mother cried. The visits to the prison were bitter
rehearsals for later failures of communication. He served
five years of the sentence and moved back to the half-blue
house. His mother had a beard and resembled a cocker

spaniel. Dog hair wafted across the floor beneath her feet and seemed to carry her along, not exactly ghostly, from room to room, slightly above the floor. The father died. The mother's hands were stained yellow from nicotine. She had recently taken a job as the Avon Lady. The animal corpse *was* a cocker spaniel, the family pet. The grass had not been mowed for nearly a decade. The house was also half-gray as if someone gave up after painting the house half-blue.

Barrel of Monkeys

One day, the barrel went quiet, and the man who owned it called the vet. The vet held his stethoscope up to the barrel and shook his head: *This is not good*, he said. *This barrel of monkeys is depressed.*

And sure enough, one by one, the monkeys climbed out of the barrel, stoop-shouldered and weary. *I've had it*, said the head monkey, *the over-crowded conditions, the same old routines. If I see one more friend of mine degrade himself by scratching under his armpits, I'll shoot myself.*

Out of a cannon? asked the man who owned the barrel, and all the monkeys fell over laughing, and the vet handed the man his bill.

4.

The Situation of the Clocks
For A. S. A.

The one in the kitchen is stuck at six p.m. as if all that
matters is the evening meal, the too-sweet scent of hya-
cinths, the sanguine odor of meat. The clock in the living
room runs counter, trying to undo itself, while the alarm
clock in the bedroom rings constantly, insisting you're not
awake. Your watch spins out of control, tightening the
band around your wrist like a tourniquet, and the clock
unwinding inside you insists it's 2:07 a.m., exact time of
your birth, as if no time has passed, and you're being
handed from doctor to nurse, held by your ankles, a poor
man's Achilles, bathed in fluorescence, surprised to be
anywhere.

Faux Pas

Flesh-driven, Christ-impaired, I stood on the outside of a glass house with a handful of stones. Inside, sanguine wax dripped down the side of a scarlet candle. A ritual of sorts commenced. The women, elegant as swans, wore masks made of jet-black feathers. The men, solid as tree trunks, wore animal skins: leopard; bear; buffalo.

I threw the stones, softly at first, to get their attention. When no one looked, I threw harder and broke the glass house into shards that fell like scimitars across their necks.

When I got home, I found the invitation in my coat pocket: *You are invited to a ritual of sorts at the glass house, tonight at eight p.m., animal attire.*

It appears I have made a mistake of grand magnitude. It is unlikely I will be invited to the next soiree.

The Happy Ending

Two rats burrow their way into his heart and build a nest. At first, it's a nuisance, all the movement as they arrange the furniture and hang their pictures. But after awhile, he gets used to it and decides not to call the exterminator. He starts to arrange his day according to the rats' movements. They are his wake up call, his dinner bell, his good night kiss.

He wishes he could take his heart out of his chest and put it on the nightstand where he could see it. He borrows a butcher knife and a small hacksaw from his neighbor and slices open his chest and cuts away at his ribcage until he can reach in to his chest and snatch out his heart. He places it on the nightstand and waits for the rats to do something. He waits for a few hours, growing more and more impatient, when he starts to doze off.

Inside his heart, the rats are very quiet, waiting for the horrible thing that has snatched their nest to go away. Without his heart, it doesn't take long for the man to die. When the rats finally get up the courage to go outside, they see the dead man on the bed. *Go inside and call your mother,* says the male rat to his wife. *Tell her there's a condominium right near us that has some vacancies.*

Glass Ceiling

The new sign for my office door finally arrived, but they
spelled "genuflect" with two n's again. Now I have to
remind everyone myself of my status, which seems de-
meaning like if you have to ask how much you can't afford
me said the hooker to the trick, and these days every
exchange reminds me of prostitution, so I was hoping the
sign would offer non-verbal assurance of some sense of
decorum, which has disintegrated rapidly over the last fifty
years or ever since the war when women joined the work
force and got some ideas of their own, and now I some-
times have to make my own lunch or go out to eat, which
unravels the moral fabric of our nation more than even the
network executives know, although the cable stations have
picked up a few threads and woven some fine programs of
interest involving video-verité, hand-held shots of cops
busting poor people for taking drugs and other activities
designed to numb them against the upstream thrust of
their existence.

But what the hell; they're on television, and that's more
than a lot of us get, who have to send our signs out again
and again to incompetents, whose lives are devoted to
usurping the quality time of guys like me, just regular guys
with better jobs than "sign misspeller," who people
depend on to make some meaning in an otherwise dog-eat-
dog world of corruption and influence, and Jesus, I'm only
the janitor, head janitor to be sure, but it's not like I run
the place, which reminds me: It's almost time to flood the
basement before the rats get back to the cafeteria.

The Last Barbecue

Madeleine had a blister at the web between her thumb and forefinger. Michael's cyst stared like a bloodshot eye from his right elbow. All the guests had some sort of injury, some hidden, some in full display. For the first half-hour, they took turns shaping hamburger into patties and yanking hot dogs from their string.

Once that was done, the host, a thin man named Tad, stood over the grill in a chef's hat cooking the meat, flipping each hamburger at just the right moment and twirling the hot dogs with his tongs. His was the most secret injury, a festering sore.

And so it went on for hours, cooking and eating, drinking and talking, displaying their stigmata. It wasn't even a special occasion. Just an ordinary Sunday. An ordinary gathering of friends. Except one thing: each loved some other's wound.

Decomposition #249

The elephant trundled with its legs in muck, while the airplane flew across the sky. For once the baker and the loaf of bread walked hand in hand down Main Street unashamed of their love, one eventually devouring the other. The night air tasted like a dill pickle.

Behind the bowling alley, kids were drinking wine with Christ. Later, a cop handcuffed himself to his mother as his crime waved in the wind like a worn flag. At last the man in the hearse woke up from his bad dream—the birth of a child that looked like him.

Suddenly all birds fell out of their trees. Only one more Sunday and this life will be over. *Oh calendar, refrain from your daily torture*, the elephant trumpeted, then disappeared.

All the rest is merely history.

Pets

The seven skinned carcasses, pink, fly-strewn, purple-veined. They knocked on the door at 4 a.m. I answered in my underwear, though considering their condition, I felt no embarrassment. I asked them, *What can I do for you?* The largest of them padded into the room, leaving a trail of bloody paw prints on my freshly mopped floor. He climbed on to the sink and drank from a dirty dish I'd left there. *Water?* I said. The other six heard me and climbed on to the sink with their leader.

I couldn't tell if they had been small dogs or another, wilder type of animal when they had fur and were alive. I walked to the cabinet and took out six dishes and filled them with cold water from the sink where their leader continued to lap up the last of the dishwater. *Would you like some fresh?* I asked him. He removed his whiskered snout from the dish and allowed me to run the water into it.

The others drank greedily from the dishes I'd placed on the floor for them. They were making a disgusting mess with their skinless husks, but I was beginning to get used to the idea of having pets and retreated to the basement to find a basket and some old blankets.

When I came back up the stairs, they were waiting at the kitchen door to be let out. I opened the door and they scurried to the breezeway and forced open the unlatched screen door.

After they were gone for about an hour, I mopped the floor, put the basket and blankets out on the breezeway and set to the task of choosing names.

The Way

The entire enterprise should take no more than two minutes. There should be a way of telling the others that will not upset them at first. Very few spectators, if any. The drawn silhouette of a horse being ridden by a man. Candles flickering in a cave. Make sure the chains are fastened tightly, but not too tight. Ask for volunteers. When the music starts, observe the other participants, surreptitiously. Pray to the god you've been trained to worship. Obtain the signature of the Lunacy Commissioner. Create the sacrifice in your own image and likeness. Eviscerate the sacrifice. It's said no one should be within three feet of you when you begin.

Vomit, California

The sun sets on the fringe of the wheat field. Mary Jane slides her nylons up her long legs, unrolling the fine silk like a snake reclaiming its shed skin. She is miles from the field, trying to remember her locker combination from senior year. The corpse lies in the middle of the field, repelling crows. Pastor Wiggins drives by in his black Continental. Dinner is on the table, steaming above a red and white checkered tablecloth. A boy, whose friends refer to him as the next James Dean, tosses a noose over a rafter in his father's barn. In the soda shoppe, the man in the long trench coat denies once again that he is from California, refutes the theory that he has anything at all to do with the film industry.

Hedda Hopper once asked Montgomery Clift to sum up his life in one sentence. *I've been knifed,* he said. His name for Los Angeles: Vomit, California. And Monty wasn't the only one who knew what it's like to be invited to a party that turns out to be a cliff above an ocean. That's the trouble with Cinemascope. It's all about perspective and light. Just ask a mirror as it gathers dust, its greatest fear.

Old Ned Chamberlain smirks and shakes his head, spins around toward the stranger on his stool. Mary Jane sidles in to the last orange booth and lifts her skirt an inch or two above her knees. *Damn flies,* she says to herself and notices five or six of the sticky rolls Hank hung from the ceiling for the purpose of killing them. She starts to cry. *Stop being so silly,* she thinks. *No one this sensitive ever made it in Tinseltown.* Hank shoots her a look that says, *You're golden, baby,* as he wipes down the counter. Now it's up to the stranger, who dunks the first half of his powdered donut in his cup of coffee, his gaze set on the flare of red in the mirror behind Hank's head.

The Betrayal

One day, in the psychiatrist's office, I told the truth, the
cage that held my heart collapsed, and my heart escaped.
The psychiatrist, in the interest of science, chose not to
catch it, or to help me repair its home. It ran into the
street, narrowly avoiding traffic, stayed for some months in
a one room apartment, developed a drug habit, couldn't
find a job or a woman, couldn't start a family.

It writes me regularly now, asks me to send money and very
little else, which I always send. It is strange without it,
quiet just before sleep when I used to listen for it to know I
was alive. Still, it was good we parted, now that I know it
needed me more than I needed it.

King of the Geese

Because it was October, the geese assembled on the lake's shiny surface, swimming beside their upside down reflections. After a few hours of gliding along, dipping their pinkish beaks in the chilly water and forming little packs, one of the geese suggested they hold an election. *We must elect our king, so that he may lead us to the promised land.* A goose of some heft, popular among the ganders, swam forward and declared his candidacy: *Elect me, my fellow geese, and I promise we will hover in the milky gray sky above this lake until eternity, legendary among geese everywhere.*

Another slenderer goose declared his intentions: *Vote for me, and I will lead us farther south than we have ever been, where there are no hunters, and the sedges and grasses float up into your beak from warm waters as green as the greenest summer leaf.*

In that moment, a third goose, tired of the commotion and empty rhetoric, flew off toward the horizon, and one by one, the other geese followed, honking, *King of the Geese, we are following.* The mad rustling of wings, fading in the clarity of the autumn sky.

Acknowledgements

I would like to thank Michael Burkard, Maile Chapman, Sean Dougherty, Dave Eggers, Paul Griner, Patrick Lawler, Rick Moody, George Saunders, and James Wagner for their support, and Keck and Parker for giving me the opportunity to publish this book. I would also like to thank Jane Mead, Lucia Perillo, and Ken Victor for their inspiration, and Philip Booth, Hayden Carruth, Stephen Dobyns, and Tess Gallagher for their encouragement.

Thanks also to the New York Foundation for the Arts, the Constance Saltonstall Foundation for the Arts, and the Cultural Resource Center of Onondaga County for their financial support during the completion of this manuscript.

About the Author

Christopher Kennedy's poems have appeared or will appear in many journals and magazines, including *Grand Street, Ploughshares, The Threepenny Review, The Quarterly,* and *Mississippi Review.* He received a Constance Saltonstall Foundation for the Arts grant in 1997 and a poetry fellowship from the New York Foundation for the Arts in 1999. One of the founding editors of the literary journal, *3rd Bed,* he is Interim Director of the MFA Program in Creative Writing at Syracuse University.